IMAGES
of America

PITTSBURGH JAZZ

IMAGES
of America

PITTSBURGH JAZZ

John M. Brewer Jr.

ARCADIA
PUBLISHING

Published by Arcadia Publishing
Charleston, South Carolina

Library of Congress Catalog Card Number: 2006937954

For all general information contact Arcadia Publishing at:
Telephone 843-853-2070
Fax 843-853-0044
E-mail sales@arcadiapublishing.com
For customer service and orders:
Toll-Free 1-888-313-2665

Visit us on the Internet at www.arcadiapublishing.com

*Dedicated to jazz artists, both past and present, who have labored
for years to develop their craft to share with the world.
Special attention has been directed towards Pittsburgh jazz as a unique
blend from years of both visiting artists and Pittsburgh artists
who collaborated and shared, both on and off stage,
new discoveries that enhanced each performance.*

CONTENTS

ACKNOWLEDGMENTS

Thanks to *New Pittsburgh Courier* and its staff for supporting the idea of presenting this book using photographs from its historic archives. Equal thanks to Carnegie Museum of Art in Pittsburgh and the staff working with the Charles Teenie Harris photograph project. Special thanks to Ernest "Tommy" Tucker who provided valuable documentation, photographs, and connection into the jazz world that existed over 60 years ago. Without his help and others from around Pittsburgh, the concepts would be incomplete. I would also like to thank Chuck Austin from 471 Music Union, Harold Young from Jazz Workshop, and Dr. James Johnson and his wife Pam Johnson from the African American Music Institute in Homewood Brushton for their observations and comments.

INTRODUCTION

This book is an overview of 20th-century jazz that emerged from Pittsburgh's African American communities between 1925 and the 1990s. The primary objective is to unveil who the artists were that influenced jazz as we know it today. To date, many jazz historians and writers credit New York City (Harlem Renaissance) artists as the driving force and point of validation when jazz lovers seek to understand more about the jazz culture. That is not to say New York City venues like the Cotton Club, Apollo Theater, and Savoy Ballroom were not featuring the best of the best artists in the world. What is presented here is an examination of where these superstars came from, and what forces and influences prompted the artists to be who they were before they took center stage in the city of lights. My primary objective in writing this book is to point out the strong relationship between Pittsburgh jazz artists and the development of modern jazz in America.

Pittsburgh artists, venues, and promoters have paved the way for others to follow. Pittsburgh's Hill district community was known as "Little Harlem" in the 1930s and 1940s. The Hill was a place with hundreds of venues committed to jazz and was utilized to promote bebop, a popular Pittsburgh form of music. One could literally walk the street and hear the crying, loving sounds from the sax play. Food joints, fresh with the smell of barbecue ribs, wings, and fries, were served with jazzy sounds that made one happy to be alive and hanging out on Wylie Avenue in the Hill district.

Artists performing in Pittsburgh's mainstream downtown venues during the 1920s and early 1930s were not African American. They soon became part of the bigger picture when they were invited uptown to the Hill. Soon downtown became uptown and uptown artists began to perform downtown. The two forces merged to the delight of Pittsburghers.

By the early 1930s, a new group of highly skilled and trained artists hit the scene. Great high school music masters had trained many of these newcomers. Mary Dawson Cardwell's opera house in Homewood Brushton served as an extra-special training ground for skilled artists and composers like Billy Strayhorn, Mary Lou Williams, and Ahmad Jamal from the city's East End communities of Homewood Brushton and East Liberty. Other communities outside of Pittsburgh, like Homestead and Duquesne, produced such greats as Maxine Sullivan and Earl "Fatha" Hines. The Hill became an important proving ground for these artists to develop and test their skills. Pittsburgh jazz became an important gateway to the north, south, east, and west. Photographs shown in this book represent a small part of who the players were that made up one of the greatest stages in the world, what we call modern jazz.

One

JAZZ LEGENDS

Bessie Smith, born in Chattanooga, Tennessee, in July 1892, is considered the "Empress of Blues." An orphan by the age of nine, she made money singing with one of her seven siblings on the streets of Chattanooga. She later accepted a challenge to sing professionally with her oldest brother. Smith was full of confidence, stage presence, and perseverance. During one show in Tennessee, when local Klansmen tried to shut her down, she confronted them with aggressiveness. The Klan members backed down and the performance went on. Smith also performed with the Fletcher Henderson Orchestra featuring J. P. Johnson and a host of young stars.

Born in New Orleans in August 1901, Louis Daniel "Satchmo" Armstrong was the greatest jazz artist of all time. His frequent trips to Pittsburgh energized aspiring artists from downtown to Duquesne. Satchmo transformed jazz with his new vocabulary of jazz phrases—tones and range on the trumpet that no one ever thought possible. Leading band members often sat in sessions attempting to learn his confusing style. He was even accused of having a modified "freak horn" that played notes not yet discovered on any scale.

Edward Kennedy "Duke" Ellington was born in Washington, D.C., in 1899. A highly intelligent and sophisticated man, he was very superstitious, charming, and perhaps the most dapper band composer that ever lived. His close relationship with Pittsburgh's Billy Strayhorn produced compositions for 28 years, and it is still impossible to distinguish where Duke stopped and Strayhorn began. Instead, they are viewed as one very big Ellingtonian force.

William (Billy) Strayhorn, born in Dayton, Ohio, in 1915, moved with his family to Pittsburgh's Homewood Brushton district in 1925. While attending Westinghouse High School, he was mentored by nationally known music director Carl McVicker. Strayhorn thrived under McVicker's influence, and he took music lessons after school at Mary Dawson Caldwell's Negro Opera House, located only blocks from school. Strayhorn became an accomplished musician and composer before he graduated. Shortly after high school he was invited to join Ellington, and for the next 28 years, he published over 200 works with him.

Errol Garner, a Pittsburgh native and jazz pianist, was born in June 1921. His family had a long music tradition, and his father and older brother, Linton, played piano. Garner wrote out his lyrics on paper, and he was never formally taught how to read music. He had a gift of literally hearing and envisioning his compositions as they appeared in his head. At all times, he carried with him paper and a sharpened pencil ready to transcribe what he heard into lyrics.

Earl Kenneth Hines, born in Duquesne in 1905, developed his skill at Schenley High School in the early 1920s. He was nicknamed "Fatha" Hines because of his mentoring skills. Hines played at every nightclub, bar, and venue in the Hill, as well as on riverboats on the Allegheny and Monongahela Rivers. He was the first pianist to develop single note, trumpet-like piano solo lines. He progressed from leading a trio to leading a large traveling band, which enabled him to recruit more musicians and popularize his music.

Ahmad Jamal, pianist and composer, hailed from Pittsburgh's East Liberty district. Born as Fritz Jones in July 1930, he joined the long list of Westinghouse High School students who later became famous musicians studying under Carl McVicker and Mary Dawson Cardwell. After forming his own group, he recorded a live album *But Not for Me*, displaying his dazzling techniques and unique use of silence that made him a dominating influence of the 1950s and 1960s.

Eleanor "Billie" Holiday was an exceptional singer who combined jazz and blues. Her music, such as "Strange Fruit" (originally a poem by Abel Meeropol), reflected painful experiences of African American victims of racial hate and discrimination, reminiscent of Bessie Smith's music in the 1920s. While touring with Count Basie in Detroit, she was asked to apply skin darkening grease to her light skin so the all-white audience would not think she was white performing with an all-black band.

Maxine Sullivan, born Marietta Williams in 1911, was one of the few black artists allowed to perform in downtown Pittsburgh's all-white clubs in the 1920s and one of the first to cohost a nationwide radio program, *Flow Gently Sweet Rhythm*. Her signature song was a classic Scottish tune "Loch Lomond." By the late 1930s, she became the foremost black female vocalist in America, inspiring young musicians like Ella Fitzgerald.

Lena Horne, born in Brooklyn, New York, in 1917, was raised in Pittsburgh's Hill district. Her exceptional beauty and delightful presence landed her a job at New York's Cotton Club as a dancer in 1934. She soon joined Noble Sissle's orchestra as a vocalist. Horne's contact with composer Billy Strayhorn improved her method of singing. Despite her rapid rise to stardom, she always seemed to return home to Pittsburgh. She is seen here celebrating her birthday at the famous Loendi Club.

David "Roy" Eldridge (left), a world-renowned trumpet player, was born in Pittsburgh in 1911. His peers called him "Little Jazz" because of his ability to play any instrument he was handed. He could also sing and compose music. Eldridge's list of credits more than exceeds perhaps any one player in the country. His legacy is full of creative improvisations, intensity, and challenges to other musicians. He loved long jam sessions and made it a practice to drill his band players to do well. Honey Boy is seen in the center.

Kenneth Spearman "Klook" Clarke, a world-class drummer, was born in Pittsburgh in 1914. He played with David Eldridge, Dizzy Gillespie, Ella Fitzgerald, Louis Armstrong, and an impressive host of other bands before forming his own. As racial discrimination raged, Clarke, also known as Kenny, joined many other black musicians who changed their names to Muslim names, claiming not to be black. Some, like Kenny, even changed their identification cards and driver's license, which reported they were "W" for white. Kenny changed his to the Arabic name Liaqat Ali Salaam.

Sarah Vaughn was accurately called "the Divine One." Her incredible virtuosity was noticed by church members from her home in Newark, New Jersey. She was formally trained on piano and organ. At age 16 she entered amateur night at the Apollo Theater and won. Pittsburgh artist Billy Eckstine recruited her to join Earl Hines's band as a vocalist and second piano. Eckstine later formed his own legendary band with a host of stars, including Dizzy Gillespie and Charlie Parker. He encouraged Vaughn to join the tour as they both explored and enjoyed a new kind of music called bebop.

15

Paul Chambers, born in Pittsburgh in 1935, will be remembered as the man who presented a revolutionary approach to bass playing. Chambers was one of the first bassists to solo, and in doing so he introduced bebop phrasing to the bass. He holds the distinction, along with John Coltrane and Wynton Kelly, of participating on two of the most important albums in jazz history: Coltrane's *Giant Steps* and Miles Davis's *Kind of Blue*.

Bebop star Charlie "Yardbird" Parker, born in Kansas City in 1920, played alto saxophone so well he influenced many trumpet, bass, and piano players. Parker denied bebop's connection to jazz and insisted it developed its own roots from a jam session in Harlem at Minton's playhouse. Parker, Dizzy Gillespie, and a trumpet player from Cleveland named Freddie Webster designed complex variations on chords to prevent unprofessional players from joining the sessions. As they explored those variations they began to shape what is known as bebop. The pioneers of this new form were Thelonious Monk (pianist), Parker, Gillespie, Kenny Clarke, Webster, and Charlie Christian (guitar).

16

Count Basie, born in New Jersey in October 1917, was an expert piano player, organist, and bandleader. Vocalists loved to play with Basie because he followed the big band tradition of featuring the singers. Some defined Basie's music as "Grits and Gravy" swing jazz. He got his nickname in Kansas City in 1926 from a radio announcer who was talking about a "royal family" of jazz. Basie later was reported to have said "Confidentially, I hated the name 'Count.' I wanted to be called 'Buck' or 'Hoot' or even 'Arkansas Fats.'"

Thelonious Sphere Monk was born in Rocky Mount, North Carolina, in October 1917. He began playing drums for a Baptist church and accompanied his mother's singing in their home in New York City. The church group became a part of a large Evangelist show that went on tour. When the troupe reached Kansas City, Monk met and was influenced by Mary Lou Williams, the Pittsburgh pianist. After returning to New York, Monk became the house pianist for the well-known Minton Playhouse in Harlem. Monk was not considered part of the bebop movement. He went his own way.

Mary Lou Williams, born in Atlanta in May 1910, moved with her family to Pittsburgh when she was four years old. By the age of five, Mary was a piano prodigy. Pittsburgh high society sent chauffeurs to East Liberty to collect "the little piano girl" to play for their teas and socials. The advanced music program at Westinghouse High School further enhanced her skills. By the age of 16 she had toured the vaudeville circuit, played with Duke Ellington's Washingtonians, and taken up with a young saxophone player named John Williams. She married him one year later. The bebop founders were all nurtured and directed by Williams.

William Clarence "Mr. B" Eckstine, vocalist, trumpet player, valve trombone player, and bandleader, was born in Pittsburgh in July 1914. Eckstine should be credited with composing and directing the first incubator band for Bebop in the country. His band featured almost all the greats. Mr. B was an extremely handsome, suave, and talented baritone singer who mesmerized the ladies from coast to coast. He was one of the first to sign a $1 million recording contract. He was deeply loved by people in Pittsburgh, particularly in the Hill, where he played clubs like the Loendi, Crawford Grill, and Hurricane.

Cabell (Cab) Calloway was born in Rochester, New York, in December 1907. A great vocalist, bandleader, and showman, his signature phrase was "hi-dee-ho." He attracted millions to his concerts and had numerous public appearances on screen or stage. Calloway gained national recognition working at the Cotton Club in New York with his band in 1932. By the late 1930s and 1940s, the Calloway band consistently stayed in the top 10 earnings in the United States. He toured internationally and appeared in musicals, movies, and concerts at home and abroad.

John Coltrane left this world on July 17, 1967, as one of the most awarded, most recorded artists in the world. Few jazz artists have influenced both modern jazz and rock artists as much as he did. Coltrane was a soprano and tenor saxophonist, composer-arranger, and undisputed avant-garde leader. In January 1965, his release of *A Love Supreme* marked the zenith of his career.

John Birks "Dizzy" Gillespie, trumpet player, vocalist, and composer, was born in Cheraw, North Carolina, in 1917. Gillespie's father was a mason who played trumpet. Gillespie started playing as a teenager and formed his own small band. After moving to New York, he played in bands with Cab Calloway, Ella Fitzgerald, Fletcher Henderson, and Duke Ellington before joining Billy Eckstine's historic bebop band tour.

Miles Davis, trumpet player, composer, and one of the original founders of bebop and Cool Jazz, had a sound that was radical and penetrating, filled with deep human emotions expressing pain, respect for the past, and love. He was born in May 1926 in Illinois to an upper-middle class family who encouraged him to learn music. In 1944, the Billy Eckstine Band played in St. Louis, and Davis was hired as a third trumpet for a few weeks. He followed the band back to New York where he accepted a scholarship to the Juilliard School. Exposure to great artists like Charlie Parker, Dizzy Gillespie, and others attracted Davis to join Parker's quintet.

Max Roach, born Maxwell Lemuel Roach on January 10, 1924, in New Land, North Carolina, was a world-class percussionist, drummer, and composer. After playing many clubs in New York City, Roach connected with Pittsburgh's Kenny Clarke, also a drummer, and played with bebop-style bands joined by Charlie Parker, Coleman Hawkins, Miles Davis, and other soon-to-be legends. Pittsburghers remember Roach as a consistent part of a dynamic duo that played at the Crawford Grill. His wife, Abbey Lincoln, was a singer, and the two frequently played together.

Coleman "Hawk" Hawkins earned the title "Father of the tenor saxophone" years after he was born in 1904 in St. Joseph, Missouri. Coleman joined other artists in New York City and toured with Fletcher Henderson. He also played clarinet and bass saxophone. Hawkins led the first bebop recording session in 1943, and he was deeply respected by his fellow musicians.

Fletcher Henderson, born in 1897 in Cuthbert, Georgia, was highly educated. He graduated from Atlanta University College in 1916 with a degree in chemistry. He later moved to New York to pursue an advanced degree and started working for the Pace Handy Music Company as a song demonstrator. Shortly thereafter, he became a recording manager for the Black Swan Recording Company. Henderson completed a few residencies at New York clubs and eventually formed his own band. His consistent stream of talent, which included his brother Horace, proved to be a valuable training ground for hundreds of artists for many years.

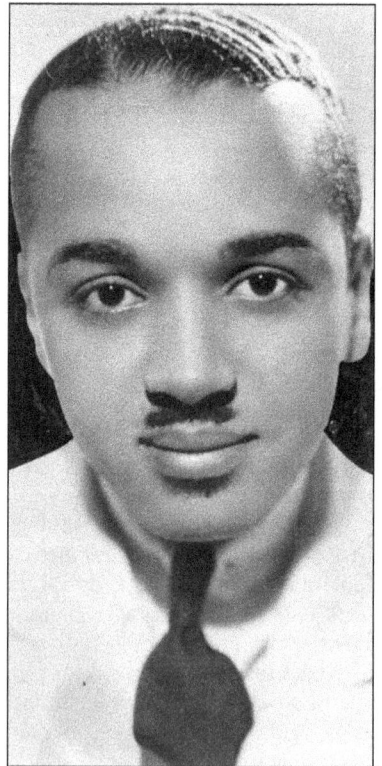

Horace Henderson, born in 1904 in Cuthbert, Georgia, was the younger brother of Fletcher Henderson. Both brothers played piano and composed and arranged music for bands. Horace arranged and composed for an impressive list of bands, including Earl Hines, Benny Goodman, Charlie Barnet, Tommy Dorsey, and Jimmy Lunceford.

Quincy Jones, born in March 1933 in Chicago, almost single-handedly carried the torch from old-school jazz legends to new school artists, despite the belief that jazz in America is deceased. Jones was raised in the tradition of great composers like Ray Charles, Dizzy Gillespie, and Miles Davis. Jones listened closely to the great artists, and he kept his hands on the pulse of the people. He listened to the stories told at the barbershops as well as the back stage sessions between the artists. Jones bridged the gap between modern jazz, rock and roll, bebop, and hip hop.

This photograph was taken by Dr. James Johnson of a young Ella Fitzgerald with her bandleader Babe Wallace. George Croft, seen to the left, was the master of ceremonies at the Cavern's Club in 1941.

Art Blakey, born in Pittsburgh on October 11, 1919, was a master drummer who came under the influence of bebop artists from Pittsburgh. Blakey shared experiences with world-renown artists like Billy Eckstine, Mary Lou Williams, Fletcher Henderson, Kenny Clarke, and Max Roach. He became a dedicated bebop drummer and helped shape the role of bebop artists around the country. Blakey was one of the coleaders of Jazz Messengers, a collective group of artists with extraordinary talent.

Nat King Cole was born Nathaniel Adams Coles in Montgomery, Alabama, in March 1919. His mother taught him to play organ until he took piano lessons at the age of 12. Cole moved to Chicago's Bronzeville neighborhood, which was known for its jazz nightclubs. The jazzy lure of artists like Earl Hines, Louie Armstrong, and others prompted young Cole to listen to this new sound, and the music inspired him. His contributions as a jazz pianist and vocalist have become a vital part of American music.

Dexter Gordan was classified as a hard bop jazz tenor saxophonist. He was also a composer, actor, and musician with intimidating sound. He played with all of the bop bands. Gordan was a big, physical man who often overshadowed part of the band. His legacy now rests in the Jazz Hall of Fame.

Erskine Hawkins (left) was born in Birmingham, Alabama, in 1914. A great composer and trumpet player, Hawkins is best known for his classic "Tuxedo Junction," a jazzy song that gained popularity during World War II. Bunny Berigan (right) was a recognizable trumpet player during the swing era.

Wynton Marsalis was a young, critically acclaimed trumpet player from a New Orleans family of jazz and blues artists. An eight-time Grammy award winner, he is known around the country as "the new voice of jazz." Some mainstream American music lovers look to Marsalis and his family to lead the movement back to jazz.

Wild Bill Davis was born in Glasgow, Missouri, in 1918. He was a jazz pianist, an organist, and an arranger of music. He became famous in jazz circles around the country for his wide-open performances that delighted crowds in the 1940s, 1950s, and 1960s.

Two

BANDS

Billy Eckstine's Band, featuring Sarah Vaughn (seated) as vocalist and Ann Baker, is pictured here. In the rear of the crowd is up-and-coming trumpet player Tommy Turrentine, the younger brother of Stanley Turrentine.

Several of the greatest bandleaders of all time, including Louie "Satchmo" Armstrong and Lionel Hampton (second from right), are pictured here. It appears the big band leaders have decided that Satchmo is the greatest of all time.

The Count Basie Band is pictured in 1964 with Basie on piano. Basie played in Pittsburgh on numerous occasions.

Pictured here is Joe Westray's famous Pittsburgh band with Joe Westray on drums. His band always managed to rock the house regardless of where they played. Westray, a businessman and an entertainer, staged concerts, band competitions, and owned a dance hall on Lincoln Avenue in Pittsburgh called Westray Plaza. Young people could go there and skate, dance, and even sing front stage. (Courtesy of the Carnegie Museum of Art, Charles Teenie Harris Collection.)

Leroy Brown's band, seen playing at Pittsburgh's Harlem Casino in the mid-1930s, included Guy F. Hunter on saxophone, George "Ghost" Howell on bass, and was led by the dapper Leroy Brown with Errol Garner on piano. Those in attendance always wore the most fashionable clothes fitting for these special occasions.

Will Hitchcock's Dream Band is pictured here playing at the Harlem Casino in the Hill in the mid-1940s. Alan "Shanks" Saunders is on tenor saxophone with Hitchcock on trombone. (Courtesy of the Carnegie Museum of Art, Charles Teenie Harris Collection.)

The Walt Harper Band, shown here on August 16, 1955, at the Crawford Grill, was always one of the most popular and versatile bands in town. They were responsible for paving the way for other black bands to play in all-white venues. Nate Harper is seen on the right and Bill Lewis is second from right. (Courtesy of the Carnegie Museum of Art, Charles Teenie Harris Collection.)

Kenny Blake on saxophone and band members Joe Harris on drums, Eric Johnson on guitar, and an unidentified bass player play upbeat jazz at the Mellon Jazz festival. (Photograph by Boyzell Mosey.)

The Roger Humphries Band is pictured here in 1996 featuring Humphries on drums and Kenny Fisher on saxophone. (Photograph by Kyle Schalow.)

The Modern Jazz Quartet is pictured here with Connie Key on drums, John Lewis on piano, Milt Jackson on vibraharp, and Percy Heath on bass. They were known for combining swing with bebop.

The Nathan Davis Band is pictured here with Davis on saxophone, Slide Hampton on Trombone, and Leon Cook in the rear on guitar.

The Jazz Workshop full band played in front of newly-opened Ramsey's II in 1992. They spread the entire band down the 7300 block of Frankstown Avenue and played for two hours straight. People abandoned their cars, buses, and bikes and sat on curbs to hear these masters of jazz play. Seen here, from left to right, are Kenny Fisher, Jaki Young, and Jose Gonzales, who make up the saxophone section of the big band. (Photograph by Dave Armaterio.)

The Al Dowe Quartet featured Etta Cox on vocals, Al Dowe on trombone, Joe "Chip" Gray on bass, Phil Costa on keyboards, and Robert Banks on drums.

The Roettes, a popular 1940s all-female band, is seen playing at the Flamingo in the Hill. Wilma Brandon is on the saxophone.

The Louis Jordan Band was one of the early bands that helped lay the foundations for bands to prosper.

34

Billy Eckstine's bebop band is pictured here in 1944. Band members from left to right are (first row) Sarah Vaughn, Billy Eckstine, John Malachi, and Connie Wainwright; (second row) Lucky Thompson, John William, Charlie Parker, Leo Parker, and Gene Amons; (third row) Chips Outcalts, Jerry Valentine, Howard Scott, and Tommy Potter; (fourth row) Marion Boone Hazel, Gail Bockman, Howard McKee, Dizzy Gillespie, and Art Blakely. (Courtesy of the Carnegie Museum of Art, Charles Teenie Harris Collection.)

Honey Boy and the Stinging Bee's with Honey Boy on vibraharp and Tommy Sewell on bass play under a tent at the veteran's hospital for a benefit in August 1971.

The Jolly Jax Trio group, who were not from Pittsburgh, were used as a comedy opening act in many of the small concerts and appearances of major stars. They often were used to loosen up the crowd before the feature act came on.

The Charles Bell Group was also popular around the Pittsburgh scene. The group featured Bell on piano, Bill Smith on guitar, Lou Mauro on bass, and Allen Blairman on drums. They were among the first bands to combine white and black artists. (Courtesy of the Carnegie Museum of Art, Charles Teenie Harris Collection.)

Kehonia Concept, one of Pittsburgh's young jazz bands, consisted of a young interracial band that developed during the high school experience at Creative and Performing Arts (CAPA) High School in Pittsburgh's East End. One of their first performances came as a result of a cross-cultural program that sponsored an equally young band from Poland. The Polish band was called Krakow. The two bands jammed at Ramsey's II jazz facility in the early 1990s. After the successful debut they accepted engagements around the city. They are Hilly Jordan on trombone, Robert Edwards on saxophone, Howie Alexander on piano, James T. Johnson on drums, and Justin Brown on bass guitar.

The David Weeks Ensemble does a good job backing up singer Sugar Cane. The band includes Curtis Lundy on bass, Vince Genova on piano, David Weeks on saxophone, and Ron Tucker on drums. (Photograph by Heather A. Cox.)

Dolphins play together at Christmas time in 1983. Everyone present was excited to hear the well-blended hot sounds from this group of young artists. Included from left to right are Fred Dolphin, Rodney McCoy, Greg Humphries, Tony Campbell, and Duane Dolphin.

The Tim Stevens Project is an excursion of jazz and pop artists who were part of the scene in Pittsburgh. Tim Stevens, a vocalist, is seated on the left.

A group of sidemen combining skills can produce a wonderful happening for the listening audience. These young men all play for nationally known jazz artists living today. They have inherited perhaps the best vibes from legends of the past. Seen here, from left to right, are (first row) Mark Schullman (drummer for Jeff Lober), Corulhus Mims (bass player for Vesta Williams), and Alee Milstein (bass player for Jeff Lober); (second row) Gerald Cooper, Rodney McCoy (electric violin), and Gary Meek (horn player for Jeff Lober).

Three

PROMOTERS AND VENUES

World-renowned music critic Leonard Feather (right) is seen here with his book on bebop. Feather wrote the book with assistance from bebop band leader Billy Eckstine. The two men pause for a moment to view the book. Eckstine's legendary band spread the new music form around the country. Feather has become the foremost expert on jazz and bebop in the 20th century.

Mother, Lillian, and sister, Viola, of famous composer Billy Strayhorn look over a music arrangement. The Strayhorns continued to help Ellington after Billy's death.

Studio Dee, located at the corner of Center and Herron Avenues, was the hottest spot in Pittsburgh to keep current about the sounds that kept the world spinning. Mary Dee, WHOD superstar deejay, could be seen in the window spinning records. The importance of this studio was enormous, as jazz and pop artists from Pittsburgh and around the country relied on this hot medium for their very existence. (Courtesy of the Carnegie Museum of Art, Charles Teenie Harris Collection.)

Mary Dee, seen here on Pittsburgh's only black station, WHOD, was a vital part of the promotion of jazz and rock records. Without her energy and fantastic popularity, jazz would have never blossomed in the city. (Courtesy of the Carnegie Museum of Art, Charles Teenie Harris Collection.)

Duke Ellington (left) is in town for a concert and interview with local radio station WWSW. Ellington is seen with the host, announcer Joe Tucker, before the performance to take time out to pump up his performance. (Courtesy of the Carnegie Museum of Art, Charles Teenie Harris Collection.)

Nat King Cole is met by hundreds of fans at the local record shop in August 1946. He signs autographs, shakes hands, and promotes his presence when he comes to Pittsburgh. Record shops in the Hill, Homewood Brushton, and downtown Pittsburgh had become the lifeblood of the industry.

Walt Harper, seated at the piano, certainly deserves credit as one of Pittsburgh's finest jazz promoters. Harper added showmanship into the mix many years ago and became connected to the mainstream of Pittsburgh cultural and corporate life.

George Wein promoted jazz in Pittsburgh and around the country. He is seen here with his wife and Duke Ellington before one of Ellington's many trips to Pittsburgh. Wein also founded and promoted jazz festivals. (Courtesy of the Carnegie Museum of Art, Charles Teenie Harris Collection.)

Back in the 1960s, Walt Harper helped to expose non–African Americans to jazz. His role as an ambassador to the mainstream was critical.

Jazz connections were made with industrial giant Gulf Oil with workshops and brief discussions about the movement of jazz into the lifestyles of mainstream Pittsburgh. Standing is the famous jazz pianist Ramsey Lewis with Walt Harper at the Hilton Hotel. Members of Gulf Scope, an employees' club, bought more than 100 tickets to attend the show. From left to right are (first row) Audrey Schlick, travel department; Pat Galaski, organization and personnel; Janet McLaughlin, travel; and Mike Strauss, David Joseph Company; (second row) Rosemary Anuskiewicz, insurance department; Lewis; Harper; Roy E. Kohler, manager special projects, public relations department; G. S. Bradley, public relations; and Michael Kumpf, tax department.

Promotion of jazz at the ballpark in Pittsburgh's Forbes Field stadium touched thousands of residents from every walk of life.

Since the late 1950s, Jazz in the Park has been one of the most popular ways to keep the jazz legacy alive and well. Harper is all smiles to be in this open venue. Pittsburgh continues to carry on this tradition by promoting Concerts in the Park during the summer months.

The big three meet and plan out performances. They are, from left to right, Walt Harper, owner of the club the Attic; Bill Colbert, public relations man for Bell Telephone Company in Pittsburgh; and Bill Powell, deejay and radio personality from the radio station WAMO (formerly WHOD).

Jazz Workshop leader Harold Young has had the task of keeping jazz alive in the city since the 1980s. Here he is seen promoting not only jazz, but Ramsey's II jazz club in Homewood Brushton in 1992. The club is located at 7310 Frankstown Avenue in the heart of one of Pittsburgh's largest black communities. Young, who is also a member of 471 Musicians Union, provides consistent entertainment at the Homewood Brushton Library.

48

Jack DeJohnette, drummer and bandleader, was part of Pittsburgh's Mellon Jazz Festival, which operated for many years during the 20th century. The festival gave local talent an opportunity to be showcased around the local clubs, bars, and food establishments.

The Pitt Jazz Festival, conducted every spring at the University of Pittsburgh, featured a large jazz concert surrounded by seminars, famous hosts, and artifacts from jazz legends from Pittsburgh.

Walt Harper breaks new ground by entering the exclusive country club scene in Westmoreland County in 1958. Harper's crew was the first black band to play the club. Two of his ardent fans are there to show support.

Pittsburgh's Harlem Casino, located in the Hill, was strongly supported by whites back in the 1940s. (Courtesy of the Carnegie Museum of Art, Charles Teenie Harris Collection.)

Jazz at Selma Burke Center in East Liberty opened up a whole new world for East End fans. Seen here, from left to right, are James Johnson on piano, Jonathan Callin on trumpet, Rodger Humphries on drums, and Herman Green on tenor saxophone. Green was the guest artist from Memphis, Tennessee.

Tony Mowod is one of the strong voices of jazz. He is seen here promoting the Mellon Jazz Festival.

Pictured playing at a local Baptist church are James Alston on saxophone, John Smith on drums, Andy Valch on keyboards, and Tom Evans on vocals. (Photograph by Don Page.)

Homewood Brushton Library is the home of Jazz Workshop.

Dr. James and Pam Johnson have been a force for promoting and educating young artists for many years. They are the owners of African American Music Institute (AAMI) in Homewood Brushton where they offer young people a great opportunity to learn how to play any instrument they like. The roots of many jazz artists today have developed from this great couple. They also feature gospel, pop, blues, or just basic lessons.

A well known face around Pittsburgh representing much of the new order of jazz artists is Joe Negri. He is an artist and spokesman for jazz artists everywhere.

Four

VOICES OF JAZZ

Phyllis Hyman, a vocalist born in Philadelphia, was raised in Pittsburgh. She was an exceptionally tall girl (six feet) with natural beauty and talent. Hyman started her career while attending Carrick High School. She was recorded in a small studio in Beltzhoover. Her dreams of becoming a famous singer began to take shape when legendary drummer Max Roach invited Nathan Davis, then head of the jazz department at University of Pittsburgh, to attend a talent show at St. Benedict the Moor Church in the Hill. Both men were amazed by Hyman's voice and poise. She continued to sing and star in musicals around Pittsburgh and elsewhere.

Dakota Staton, born in Pittsburgh in June 1931, also attended Westinghouse High School. By the age of 16, she was chosen as a vocalist and appeared with Joe Westray's big band in Pittsburgh. After a few years with Westray and trips to Detroit, Canada, Indianapolis, Cleveland, and St Louis, she moved to New York City to seek recognition as a singer, although she never got her big break.

Carmen McRae is considered a brilliant vocalist and accomplished piano player. Her legacy comes from her phrasing and use of lyrics for some of the biggest names in 20th-century jazz. Billie Holiday was the vocalist who influenced her to sing and compose. It was reported she once said, "If Billie Holiday hadn't existed, I probably wouldn't have, either." Her connection in Pittsburgh came through her marriage to Pittsburgh's native son and world-famous drummer, Kenny Clarke. Although the couple eventually parted ways, McRae's introduction to bebop through her husband never dissolved.

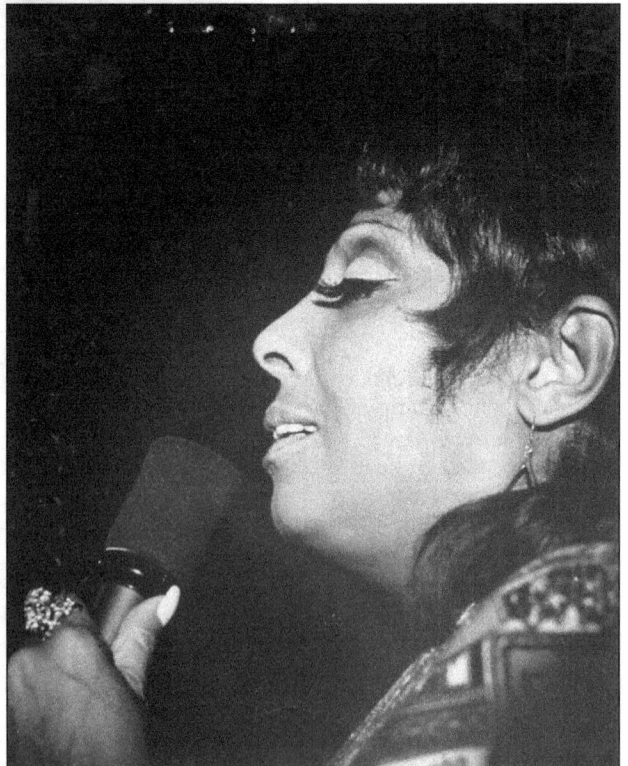

Tiny Irvin, seen here at one of the local clubs in Pittsburgh, had a huge following of supporters who loved her performances. She performed with big bands and small combos in concerts with superior stage presence. (Courtesy of the Carnegie Museum of Art, Charles Teenie Harris Collection.)

Jewel Brenner was everything jazz lovers wanted to experience. She was exciting to watch. She is seen here with a small band that included Gordan "Slick" Jackson on piano, Billy Stewart on guitar, and J. C. Gordan on tenor saxophone. (Courtesy of the Carnegie Museum of Art, Charles Teenie Harris Collection.)

Hazel Dorothy Scott was born in the June 1920. A jazz and classical pianist and singer, she played bebop, blues, and ballads. Scott was very popular in Pittsburgh, playing many of the Hill clubs, including the Crawford Grill, where she is pictured. She was married to powerful congressman Adam Clayton Powell for 11 years. Scott was the first African American woman to have her own show. Her show the *Hazel Scott Show*, aired only for a brief period because of her open opposition to Sen. Joseph McCarthy and her views on racial segregation.

Ella Fitzgerald is pictured during the start of her long career as a vocalist.

The incomparable Sarah Vaughn (right) is pictured in New York being visited by one of her great admirers, Marilyn Maxwell.

Seldom talked about but a force during her time was Una Mae Carlise. She was a beautiful and extremely talented singer and pianist. Before Billie Holiday, Carlise's style, hair dressing, and approach to jazz was influenced by most of the jazz greats in the 1920s and 1930s. This photograph was taken in 1942.

Nancy Wilson has great style, look, and a smooth presence that let everyone know she is a jazz vocalist. Her visits to the Pittsburgh scene started many years ago at Walt Harper's place. She has worked with another smooth artist, Ramsey Lewis, who also appeared at Harper's place back in the early 1980s. She has recorded many hit songs and was inducted into the Jazz Hall of Fame in 1999.

Etta Cox was originally from St. Joseph, Missouri, although she has lived in Pittsburgh for many years. A highly educated vocalist, actress, and poet, she performs and educates young people through music. She has been recorded and often invited to appear around the Pittsburgh region.

Five

MENTORS AND STUDENTS

Ozanam Strings, an entire orchestra consisting of young people, has served as a mentor to thousands of aspiring area musicians. The foundation of the organization is from the Catholic Church charity St. Vincent De Paul, founded by 19th-century French Roman Catholic scholar Antoine Fre'der'ic Ozanam (1813–1853). Many local artists began their formal training in the musical center located in the Hill. Sister Francis is seen conducting one of many sessions with the gifted young musicians.

Popular singer and guitar player George Benson is seen here with deejay and radio personality Mary Dee Goode. Benson was a very young man when he was introduced into the Pittsburgh scene. Mentors like Goode provided guidance for this popular hometown player.

AAMI is located on Hamilton Avenue in Homewood Brushton. AAMI founders, Dr. James and Pam Johnson, provide unique mentoring and instructions for young people to learn any instrument. Here Sandy Dowe, vocalist, is accompanied by Ron Fudli on bass, Ralph Guzzi on trumpet, and James on keyboard.

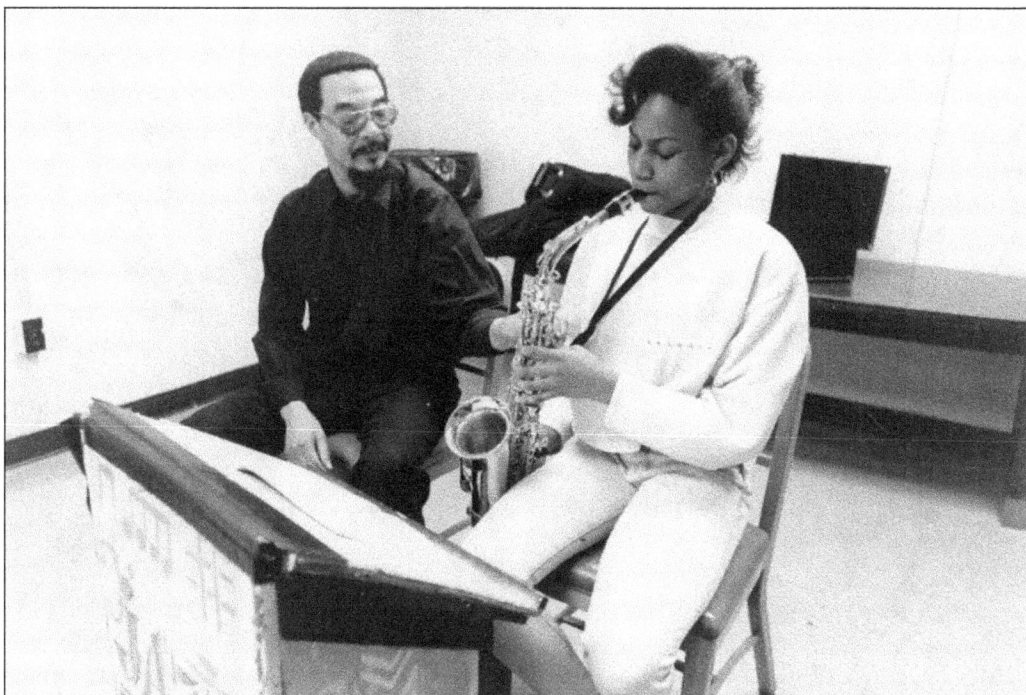
Top saxophone player Kenny Fisher is seen giving instructions to a young lady learning how to play the saxophone.

Ramsey's II, a jazz club located in Homewood Brushton, was the site chosen to debut a young jazz ensemble from Poland. These ladies are members of the Krakow Youth Ensemble's keyboard section. They are, from left to right, Magoa Wojcik, Magda Zieba, and Agata Ptasnik. They have spent most of their careers studying jazz bands from America. (Photograph by Dave Aromatoro.)

CAPA High School students play with the Krakow Youth Ensemble. These players later formed their own band called Kehona Concept. From left to righ they are Hilly Jordan on trombone, Robert Edwards on saxophone, Howie Alexander on piano, James T. Johnson III on drums, and Justin Brown on bass saxophone.

Charles "Poogie" Bell, son of bandleader Charles Bell, plays the drums. He is one of many fortunate youth to come from a musical family that encouraged him to join the family tradition. Seen in this photograph from May 22, 1965, Poogie is only three years old. He later went on to play with some great names from Pittsburgh and around the country.

"Lucky" Peterson is a young man with determination and focus, as can be seen from this photograph from December 18, 1971.

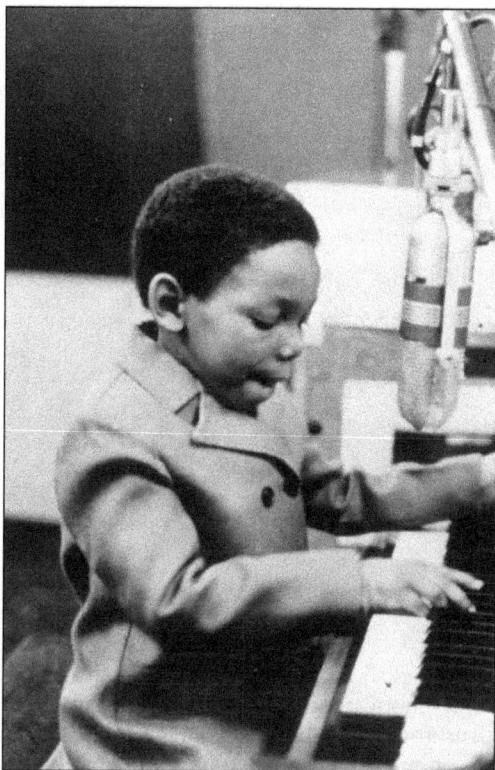

Anthony Rucker plays the trombone at an early age.

Jazz Workshop of Pittsburgh performs to a whole host of people. They conduct seminars to high school students, as well as holding regular meetings at the Carnegie Library in Homewood Brushton. Seen here are director Harold Young and Jose Gonzales playing the saxophone. (Photograph by Scola.)

Harry T. Burleigh (1866–1949) may be considered a master composer, arranger, and great teacher of all music styles. Burleigh was a soloist who was raised in Erie. During his long and productive career, he was a voice instructor for world-famous singers Paul Roberson and Marian Anderson. His spirituals and ballads, which were based on cries from slavery, have been part of the foundation of music performed by African Americans during the 20th century.

Pittsburgh jazz artist, instructor, historian, and photographer Nelson Harrison has played a major role in supporting jazz education and promoting jazz traditions passed down from ancestors. He has played with large bands around the country. A trombonist by training, Harrison is a graduate and former student of famous music instructor Carl McVicker from Westinghouse High School. His connections to university programs in the city serve as a vital link to the Pittsburgh scene.

Mary Lou Williams, known as a jazz legend, mentored the best of the best jazz and bebop artists in the country.

Charlotte Catland, former recreation director at Washington Playground, provided instruction in voice and piano to young developing talents like Billy Strayhorn back in the 1930s. She deserves more attention for her contributions to artists in Pittsburgh. She is seen here in the early 1930s giving voice lessons to young people.

Six

PITTSBURGH FAVORITES

George Benson was first known as a jazz guitarist who was born in March 1943 and raised in the Hill. His long career as an entertainer began when he was eight years old and has produced eight Grammy awards, hit rhythm and blues records, and respect among other musicians in America. Benson is a friendly man who represents what every generation would call "cool, very cool." His early life in the Hill found him surrounded by other great young jazz artists. After years as a rhythm and blues king, his latest sounds have returned to jazz. Benson was, and still is, one of the big favorites in his hometown.

Dwayne Dolphin, a Pittsburgh bassist, is everything one expects out of a bass player. He is a big man with a powerful expression. Influenced by Paul Chambers, Stanley Clarke, and Bootsey Collins, Dolphin apprenticed with some of the masters. He is also a music educator and composer. Dolphin's latest release, *Ming*, features jazz classics and original compositions.

Rodney McCoy is a Pittsburgh-raised young man from a family packed with musical talent. His parents, uncles, and aunts could sing, play music, and pack a church on Homewood Avenue with hundreds of loyal supporters ready to hear the sounds from the McCoy and Darkins combo. McCoy was the first in Pittsburgh to introduce listeners to an electric violin. Over 40 years, ago he calmly walked into Karl's Kork and Keg on the corner of Kelly and Dallas Avenues and began to play. By the end of his first 15-minute set, people were clapping and standing on chairs to see who he was.

Donna Davis, a Pittsburgh keyboard player, is a good musician. She is full of positive energy, soulful, and one of the reasons why many local jazz bands still create excitement in a city that can no longer to be considered jazz central.

Herbie Mann, a jazz flute player, was considered by many to be one of the greatest flute players in the world. Mann was known as an artist who expanded his musical rhythms to blend harmonies from Africa, Japan, Jamaica, and Brazil. He recorded with other internationally known artists.

Kenny Garrett is an alto saxophone player who has earned a reputation as a great composer and entertainer. He is seen playing at the popular Pittsburgh spot Rosebud. Garrett has delighted diverse crowds with his energetic performances. He has appeared with Gil Scott Herron, Maceo Parker, Rodney McCoy, and many other well-known jazz and pop artists. (Photograph by Victor Scott.)

Sandy Dowe, local Pittsburgh vocalist, is a teacher of music. She has taught at CAPA High School and Helen Faison School. She is seen here with her quartet at the Cotton Club.

This father and daughter combination features Al and Sandy Dowe at the Trolley Station Oral History Center. John Garrick is on keyboards.

Stanley Turrentine, born in Pittsburgh in April 1934, was encouraged to play music at an early age. By the age of seven he was playing piano. Turrentine and good friend Ahmad Jamal practiced together at Turrentine's Hill district home. By the time he was in high school, Turrentine formed a band with his brother, Tommy, a trumpeter. The team of inspired players worked several local spots, including Perry's Bar, high school proms, and local parties. He ascended through the ranks of arts, often as a sideman, gaining experience with some of the biggest names in jazz.

Kenny Blake, a world-class jazz saxophone player from Pittsburgh, may be one of the most popular artists in this city. Blake has infused the great past styles of jazz, blues, bebop, and pop music and blended them into his own expression. Today, Blake may be seen around Pittsburgh in a host of different settings. He has recorded and recently released a CD sure to enhance his already immense popularity. The great legends of jazz would be proud to see the tradition still alive and well in the 'Burg.

The Spider Rondnelli Quartet consists of Curtis Lundy on bass, David Weeks on saxophone, and popular entertainer Arnold "Spider" Rondnelli on vocals.

Seven

MAGICAL FINGERS

Errol Garner and his older
brother, Linton, possessed the
magic touch. Born and raised
in Pittsburgh, the brothers
have traveled around the world
spreading the music that unites
men together. Linton spent
most of his career in Canada as
house artist at many of the great
spots, while Errol made many
appearances on television, in
concert ballrooms, and elsewhere.

Earl "Fatha" Hines's magic was spread throughout the country with his bebop bands, influence on other artists, and his many years of contact with just about every facet of life. His fans come from every race, color, and religion. He is seen here with a glamorous rooting section in Texas. His good looks, sharp dressing style and smile, combined with his tremendous playing ability made him one of the best artists to come out of Pittsburgh.

Nat King Cole is seen here sharing a moment with amateur singer and former light heavyweight champion of the world, Sugar Ray Robinson. Cole was known for his smooth fluid playing and soft irresistible voice. His magic is everlasting and a vital part of American music from the 20th century.

James Price Johnson (1891–1955), known as J. P., was considered to be the "Father of Stride." He played jazz piano using his right hand to play the melody while the left hand alternated between a single note and a chord played an octave higher. Johnson was an important link between ragtime and jazz music, and his influence on legendary artists like Duke Ellington, Fats Waller, and Thelonious Monk has been documented by jazz historians. He is pictured here playing one of the night spots in the Hill with his trademark cigar. (Photograph by Sockwell.)

Eubie Blake, born in Baltimore, Maryland, in 1887, lived until February 1983. A composer and pianist, Blake played jazz, ragtime, and any popular music in demand. Blake was the first African American to compose a Broadway musical, *Shuffle Along*, in 1921.

Carl Arter (1918–2006) was raised on Pittsburgh's North Side. Arter was an accomplished pianist and saxophonist, as well as a leader in Pittsburgh's jazz community. President of the American Federation of Musicians local 471, he dedicated much of his life to teaching music while still playing with some of the jazz greats. Chuck Austin, the current president of 471 union is quoted as saying, "He was an unheralded genius. He was a master musician in terms of harmony and arranging music." Andy Fite is seen on guitar.

Ahmad Jamal (standing), one of Pittsburgh's greatest jazz legends, is seen with friend and fellow artist Sonny Stitt in 1969, signing a performance contract that started a national tour for Jamal, the famous East Liberty artist.

Pittsburgh's own Walt Harper (far left) deserves special attention for his magical hands and ability to pave the way for young jazz artists like Jamal (second from left). Harper's influence on the jazz scene during the 20th century qualified him as an icon. He grew up in the Schenley Heights section of the Hill, and formed a 10-piece band. He was nicknamed "the Prom King" because of the many proms that the band played at. Harper became a hit at Pittsburgh's famed Crawford Grill and other spots around the region. He also opened a downtown club called the Attic, which further enhanced his popularity at home.

Gene Ludwig, a popular Pittsburgh jazz organist, was often hidden from the limelight he deserved. He was often called upon to play with the big stars when they came to Pittsburgh. He is a quite humble man, who sat in the background wailing away on his keyboards. Ludwig, who was born and raised near Pittsburgh, was trained as a classical pianist at a young age. He is seen here playing with blues singer Chismo Charles Anderson and drummer Roger Humphries at the Shadyside Arts Festival. (Photograph by Heather A. Cox.)

Johnnie "Hammond" Smith is one of
many artists playing the instrument
that give him his nicknamed. The
Hammond B-3 organ became an
instrument of choice by the top jazz
artists. Born in Louisville, Kentucky,
in December 1933, his real name is
John Robert Smith. Smith learned
piano as a child, and after moving
to Cleveland and hearing jazz organ
pioneer Wild Bill Davis, he switched
from piano to organ. Years later
he mastered the Hammond B-3
organ and gladly accepted his new
nickname. Smith is pictured seated at
his namesake, the Hammond organ.
(Photograph by George West.)

Billy Taylor, born in Greenville, North
Carolina, in 1921, is an extremely well
educated artist, composer, and educator
of music. Taylor is respected worldwide.
His frequent trips to Pittsburgh featured
him playing at Walt Harper's Attic in
the Market Square district of downtown
Pittsburgh. His long list of awards and
degrees are only preceded by his musical
presentations on piano.

Nancy Taylor is seen here playing keyboards with her group. She is all business on the keyboards providing listeners with top-notch entertainment regardless of where she plays.

The string section of Earl "Fatha" Hines's band, seen here, was a vital part of Hines's major band.

Eight

GIVE THE DRUMMER SOME

Bernard "Buddy" Rich, born in Brooklyn, New York, in 1917, was an American jazz drummer and bandleader. Known as a drummer with tremendous speed combined with improvisation techniques, Rich was said to be one of the best drummers in the world. His rise to fame started during his childhood. Rich was influenced by Gene Krupa, Chick Webb, and Jo Jones. He played with Tommy Dorsey's band, Benny Carter, Les Brown, and other top bands before organizing his own band. Rich was known to be quick tempered, emotional, and passionate about his music and band member's performances.

On January 15, 1909, Gene Krupa was born in Chicago. Krupa's parents were very religious and full of expectation that he would become a priest. He attended St. Joseph College for one year until his strong love for the drums caused him to drop out and follow his desire to become a great drummer. He is seen here at one of his many performances in Pittsburgh.

Harold Jones, born and raised in Richmond, Indiana, was a drummer who played with all of the big names in jazz. After a long and successful career of recording and playing drums, he taught others how to interpret music on drums. Seen here in April 1967, Jones is warming up before making an appearance in Pittsburgh.

Pittsburgh's own Joe Harris is a highly energetic, deeply motivated drummer who seems ageless. His familiar smiling face and quick steps can be traced to every jazz venue that has opened its doors in Pittsburgh.

Cecil Brooks II, a Pittsburgh native, is known as a seasoned veteran who is well respected in the jazz community. His style of playing is smooth and always in touch with the band. Brooks has played with the best artists in the country. He plays local venues of all types and is a musical mentor for young artists, including his now-famous son, Cecil Brooks III.

Cecil Brooks III, son of Cecil Brooks II, has toured worldwide with his aggressive, creative style of playing drums. Seen here playing at Ramsey's II jazz club in Homewood Brushton, Brooks puts on a show that fans seldom forget.

Roger Humphries is a master percussionist, bandleader, and mentor for young people in Pittsburgh. He has kept the tradition of big bands alive. Seen here playing at the Shadyside Arts Festival in 1989, Humphries knows how to put on a show.

Cecil Washington, from Homewood Brushton, has played with every style of band regardless of their music. Washington is always on the road playing with artists like Santana and others who demand to have the best.

Muhammad Idris puts on a great solo act. He always made sure to "give the drummer some." Known around Pittsburgh and elsewhere as a highly involved drummer and crowd pleaser, he is seen here entertaining a crowd in November 1981.

Pola V. Roberts (right) was born in August 1936, in Pittsburgh, and raised in the Hill district. She was a self-taught drummer who started tapping beats on any surface. This compulsion to drum prompted her to play bongo and eventually the drums. By the age of 17, she became a drummer. Gloria Coleman, a female bandleader, discovered Roberts and hired her to play for her all-female band. She later moved to New York and played with such greats as Stanley Turrentine, Max Roach, Art Blakely, George Benson, and Jack McDuff.

Nine

STARS OF THE HORNS

Miles Davis
and Roy "Little
Jazz" Eldridge
were two
super masters
of the horn.
They both
were defiant,
creative, and
consistent with
establishing
new levels for
others to follow.

Roy "Little Jazz" Eldridge and Harry Lim came from two different worlds, and yet, they eventually met and played together on January 25, 1941. Eldridge was from the streets of Pittsburgh and spent most of his time around some of the greatest jazz artists playing in the city. Lim was born in Batavia and raised on the other side of the world in Jakarta, Indonesia. Lim was influenced by jazz while living in the Netherlands. Jazz music eventually lured him to come to America in 1939, and he became a producer of jazz, bop, and swing all-stars. Eldridge wanted to be the best trumpet player in the world, and Lim wanted to produce the best small group in the world. Both men were highly successful. Seen here Little Jazz gives Lim some pointers on the trumpet.

Sonny Rollins, seen on the left, and Donald Byrd represented a separation from bands that only featured one outstanding player. Jazz fans were delighted to hear two or more masters playing together, sharing stage time, and displaying open admiration for each other's abilities. Rollins and Byrd certainly were the best.

Benny Bailey, Johnnie Griffin, Nathan Tate Davis, and Mikhail Alperin, seen here from left to right, created a whirlwind of sound capable of literally knocking fans off their feet. This double duo combines four men with diverse backgrounds together creating an unforgettable moment on stage. Bailey, a trumpeter from Cleveland, played bop style. He spent most of his career in Europe and the Netherlands. Griffin, from Chicago, was an aggressive saxophone player who dazzled his fans with his speed. He loved to form duel jam sessions with other players. Davis, born in Kansas, spent six years in Paris mastering the saxophone. After the military and Europe, he moved to Pittsburgh and became a professor of music at the University of Pittsburgh. He also became the director of the jazz studies department at the university. Alperin, a jazz pianist, was born in the Ukraine in 1956. He plays Melodica and sings.

World-famous trumpet player Dizzy Gillespie (left) plays with world-renowned saxophone player Davis.

New links to keep the music alive in Pittsburgh were established with jam sessions, jazz festivals, and progressive venues around the city. Seen here is Rodger Barbour (above) at a jazz jam session conducted at the Hill district's Hill House on Center Avenue. Barbour has ensured younger players like fellow trumpeter Darryl Cogdell (below) continue the tradition. Cogdell is seen playing with the Jazz Workshop in Homewood Brushton in front of Ramsey's II jazz venue in 1992. (Photograph by Dave Anaratono.)

This double duo performing at the Aragon Ballroom in downtown Pittsburgh in 1944 features, from left to right, Luck Thompson, Dizzy Gillespie, Charlie Parker, and Billy Eckstine. (Courtesy of the Carnegie Museum of Art, Charles Teenie Harris Collection.)

The ultimate couple playing bebop are Charlie Parker (second from left) and Dizzy Gillespie (second from right). They have been considered by many as the heart and soul of the bebop movement.

Howard McGhee played with Miles Davis early in his career. Born in Detroit in 1918, McGhee was the first jazz bebop trumpeter and was known to have very fast fingers. McGhee was also the first to introduce bebop in California in 1946.

Louis Jordan was, after Armstrong and Ellington, perhaps the most influential bandleader of his time. He was known as "King of the Jukebox" and was one of the first black artists to have both white and black supporters following his jazz, blues, and boogie-woogie tunes. Born in Brinkley, Arkansas, in 1908, he took up alto saxophone after learning the clarinet and piano. He also was a great vocalist, songwriter, and entertainer. Jordan's influence on popular music is significant, as some say he invented rock and roll. Even the "Godfather of Soul," James Brown, once replied when asked about the Jordan influence, "Oh, in every way: he could sing, he could dance, he could play, he could act. He could do it all."

J. J. Johnson was a master trombonist who was able to play the more cumbersome and awkward trombone with great speed and control. He played the innovations by Charlie Parker and Dizzy Gillespie on slide trombone better than any other trombonist. Born in Indianapolis in 1924, Johnson's career included playing with Count Basie's orchestra, Illinois Jacquet, Miles Davis, and Charlie Parker.

Eddie Harris came from Chicago where he was born in 1924. Harris came under the influence of famous Captain Walter Dyette, a black leader who was directly responsible for guiding the careers of young artist in the 1930s, 1940s, 1950s, and early 1960s. After high school, Harris entered the military where he polished his skills as a saxophone player while on tour with the Seventh Army Band. Returning to America, he was the first to introduce electro voice creation for the Selmer Instrument Company. His recordings have featured his electric saxophone.

Willis Jackson, nicknamed "Gator" because of his birthplace, Miami, Florida, was born on April 25, 1932. Jackson joined the Duke Ellington band as a teenager. He played as a sideman for many years in bands that were recording. Jackson is credited with starting the jazz soul movement in the late 1950s. During that time, artists like Jack McDuff and others became famous.

Queen Ingrid Cook, from Monessen, entered the jazz scene by winning a local pageant in 1991. The queen wears her crown well and was expected to continue playing her saxophone in Pittsburgh.

Stanley Turrentine, from Pittsburgh's Hill district, is the undisputed "King of Saxophone" in this city. He and his brother Tommy both have contributed to Pittsburgh jazz for many generations. Stanley is seen here playing in 1997 at the 10th annual Hill District Community Development Corporation event. (Photograph by Chris Lowry.)

Pittsburghers are happy Nathan Davis decided to make this city his home. His contributions to jazz at the University of Pittsburgh, CAPA, Manchester Craftsmen Guild, and other local venues cannot be measured in one book or article. Davis is seen in 1981 displaying his talent as a master saxophonist.

Tony Campbell is a local saxophone player and well-known entertainer around Pittsburgh. This photograph was taken in February 1982 at one of Campbell's many appearances.

Vinard Studios

Harold Betters, sometimes called "Mr. Trombone" has touched jazz lovers for the past 40 years. Betters and his brother Jerry, who is also a jazz artist, are from Connellsville. Harold performed at Pittsburgh's top jazz clubs such as the Crawford Grill, Encore, and Holiday House. He even played for some of the Pittsburgh Steelers football games. This photograph was taken in October 1966 to promote a session at the Crawford Grill.

Stan Getz, tenor saxophone player, was born in Philadelphia. Getz was one of the most influential players in America having played with legendary bandleaders like Jack Teagarden, Stan Kenton, Benny Goodman, and Jimmy Dorsey just to name a few. He is world traveled and well based in understanding Brazilian and Latin rhythms. The list of artists who have learned from Getz is impressive and historic.

James Moody has played the Pittsburgh scene for many years. His popularity among devout jazz lovers has lasted for many decades.

Arnett Cobb was born in Houston, Texas, in 1918. He played piano and violin before becoming a tenor saxophone player. He played with Lionel Hampton for five years from 1942 to 1947. Cobb's career as an artist was interrupted for many years due to illness and a car crash. He did tour Europe, however, in the 1970s.

Jackie McLean is seen playing at the Pitt Jazz Festival in 1997. McLean is an alto saxophone player with an extensive background. He was mentored by jazz greats like Charlie Parker and Thelonious Monk.

Kenny Powell and his quartet provide quality music for local Pittsburgh venues and private parties for local clients. They have performed at Pittsburgh's Renaissance Hotel in downtown Pittsburgh and a host of other venues in the region.

Kenny Fisher is a Pittsburgh native, having grown up in the Hill district. His life has been dedicated to the jazz culture in Pittsburgh. A popular saxophone player, he has played with just about every jazz band that performs in the city. He is a great mentor and role model for aspiring artists.

David Weeks plays the local scene in Pittsburgh. Weeks formed his own band and gained popularity among Pittsburghers.

Well-known trombone player Grover Mitchell was born in Whatley, Alabama, but he was raised in Pittsburgh where he attended Westinghouse High School. After leaving high school he joined the Duke Ellington band. During his successful career, Mitchell wrote music for motion pictures. He is best known for music that was used in the movie *Lady Sings the Blues*.

Paul Desmond, a jazz saxophone player, appeared in Pittsburgh frequently. Best known as the saxophonist for Dave Brubeck's quartet, Desmond's famous single "Take Five" was the first of its kind to sell one million records.

Ten

MEMORIES

Seen here is a master practice session with Ella Fitzgerald, Louie Armstrong, and Sy Oliver.

Count Basie's final appearance at Syria Mosque in Pittsburgh occurred on August 4, 1983. (Photograph by McMillian.)

Jazz organist Charles Earland is seen playing at the Shadyside Arts Festival. Erland is accompanied by O'Donnell Levy on guitar and Ron Tucker on drums.

Billy "Mr. B" Eckstine appeared around the world charming fans with his great looks and wonderful baritone voice.

Duke Ellington poses with the Brownie sisters while in Pittsburgh in May 1940.

Duke Ellington continues sharing his joy with the ladies while visiting Chicago.

The Nat King Cole Trio appeared at the Crawford Grill, Hurricane, and other venues in Pittsburgh. Oscar Moore is seen on the right and Cole is in the center.

This legendary Louie Armstrong poster was created to help support the March of Dimes.

The short-lived but popular Dizzy's Club was located in the strip district of Pittsburgh. Appearing were Dave Budway on piano, Dwayne Dolphin on bass, Chico Freeman on saxophone, and Winard Harper on drums. (Photograph by T. Jefferson.)

How can one forget the Ink Spots, who are shown in this photograph from August 31, 1940.

Local great, Marcus Kelly, plays at the Crawford Grill in the Hill district of Pittsburgh.

Famous jazz and blues pianist Jay McShann plays with Bobby Boswell on bass and John Eskridge on drums at the Shadyside Arts Festival.

The nationally traveled Jazz Preservation Band from New Orleans plays at Heinz Hall in Pittsburgh in March 1977.

Singer Jimmy Rushing was fondly nicknamed "Five by Five" by his peers.

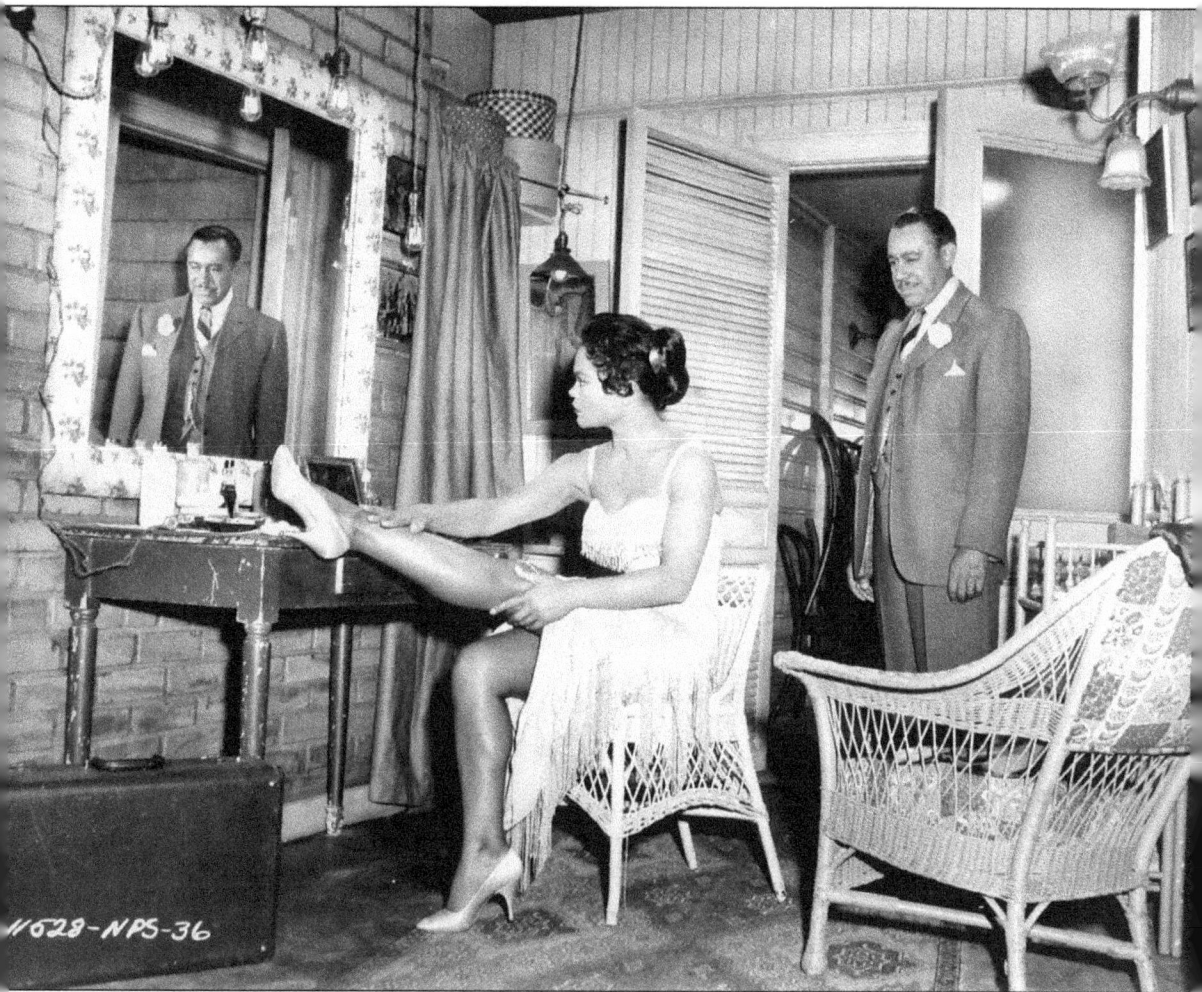

Actress Eartha Kit appears with Cab Calloway in the production of *St. Louis Blues.*

Dizzy Gillespie and Lionel Hampton enjoy some friendly horseplay in the dressing room before going on stage.

Louie Armstrong was having fun,
whether he was playing tricks or
sharing drinks with other artists.

Billie Holiday and her husband enjoy some downtime on the beach in Atlantic City.

The big three beboppers, from left to right, Sarah Vaughn, Billy Eckstine, and Dizzy Gillespie were the heart of Eckstine's 1944 bebop band.

118

The ageless beauty of Lena Horne is seen here.

Ella Fitzgerald and Count Basie pose for this picture while out for drinks together.

Ella Fitzgerald performs her trademark song, "Tiskit a Taskit," in 1940.

Count Basie (left) shares a moment with famous author Richard Wright while in France.

Louie Armstrong sings with Velrica Middleton in 1971.

This classic photograph captures famous actor Jimmy Stewart (right) and Louie Armstrong (center) sharing tips.

Seen here is popular recording artist Freddie Hubbard.

123

Duke Ellington poses with Ivy Anderson (left) and Mary Dee Goode while visiting Pittsburgh.

Dinah Washington is known as one of the most popular and versatile singers of all time.

The imposing brilliant saxophonist Sonny Rollins is pictured here.

The beautiful, energetic singer Phyllis Hyman poses with her drummer.

Earl "Fatha" Hines is shown posing in his convertible.

"Old Black Magic" singer Billy Daniels poses for this photograph in September 1970.

This early photograph of "Lady Day," otherwise known to the world as Billie Holiday, was taken in the 1930s.

Visit us at
arcadiapublishing.com